The Plastic Devil

The Plastic Devil

Raymond Vasquez

To order additional copies of this book, contact:
Xlibris Corporation
1-888-795-4274
www.Xlibris.com
Orders@Xlibris.com
125572

CONTENTS

CHAPTER 1

Interest Is a Killer

We all work hard for our money for a better living—to pay bills, to buy nice things, to eat. We work, we get paid, then we proceed to spend the cash that we have earned. Some of us spend the cash we are going to earn in the future now, and that's where the interest kicks in, and that item you just purchased on credit is costing you a lot more than what it really should. The definition of *interest* is "a charge for the use of credit or borrowed money." Just think, if you can actually save some cash and borrow from yourself when you need to, you don't have to pay a charge to borrow your own money.

Interest is a killer. The only item that you should be paying interest on is your house because you don't have $400K lying around. Apart from that, you shouldn't pay interest on anything else, absolutely anything else. Every time you pay interest, you are taking away your weekly paycheck and chopping off a part of it. I will explain.

If you are earning $400 a week and have to pay on a weekly basis a bill that has an interest fee of $40, automatically, your $400 becomes $360. You just flushed $40 of your hard-earned paycheck down the toilet 'cause you purchased something with credit and needed to pay the interest. So before you make the next purchase on credit, calculate how much of your paycheck you are kissing away, and determine if you can actually wait until you have cash to buy the item outright without having to pay any interest. Stop purchasing items on credit, calculating that you will pay them with your next check because one week becomes another week, and $100 becomes $5,000. All of sudden, you're paying half your paycheck on interest, and then how are you supposed to get ahead if half of your month's salary is gone? You might just able to make ends meet and cover the rest of your expenses—your rent, cable, coned weekly lunch money.

Interest is an unnecessary evil and a real killer.

Learn, at an early age in your life, to buy things when you can with cash and to stretch your hard-earned dollar as much as possible. Try to live for two weeks with your salary and save the cash for another two weeks. Therefore, you will always have a nice stash—a nice savings for future needs.

CHAPTER 2

Society: Systems to Keep Us Going in Circles

The society that we live in today has a lot of systems in place to keep us going in circles. Have you ever gone around a block in your car and around? Do you really get anywhere or you stay in the same place no matter how many times you go around that block? You are still in the same block, right?

The society we live in thinks it is normal for us to owe an average of 20k on credit cards, owe $40K on a car, owe $80K on student loans, go on vacations on credit, buy time-shares we don't need, buy furniture we can't afford, refinance our homes to do unnecessary upgrades, and pay for loans we should have never taken in the first place. Our society has systems in place to keep us broke, to keep us down, and to keep us from progressing in life. How are we supposed to get ahead with all these systems in place to help us get all these nice things so that we can pay interest for the rest of our lives? From day one, we were set up to fail.

I have news, for my parents raised me to buy what I can with green cash or don't buy it at all.

It is not normal for you to take all these loans—student loans, car loans, credit card loans—so that by the time you get out of college, you are already $150K in the hole. No no no.

Is this the American way? Well, there has to be another way to get the things you want and need without getting into so much debt.

We need to learn at an early age the difference between wanting or needing something. For instance, I want a BMW but I need a car. So do I finance a BMW and pay for the interest for five years, or do I buy a $4,000 Toyota for now and pay zero interest? Differentiate between your wants and needs. Learn this early, and it will save you thousands and thousands of dollars.

CHAPTER 3

Credit Cards: The Plastic Devil

The reason why credit cards are the plastic *devil* is that while you are in college, you start getting credit card offers. Since you are naive, you get a card and start shopping, buying things you don't need, and before you know it, you owe $10K on credit cards with an interest of 20 percent, which to me is almost loan-sharking and should be illegal.

Before someone under twenty-five gets a credit card, they should go to counseling. They should pass a class that explains to them the dangers in owning a credit card.

If you didn't have a credit card, you will either wait until you save up the cash to buy that item or get someone else to buy it for you or not buy it at all.

It is so easy to go to a shoe store. You will definitely find a new pair of Kicks you absolutely must have, and then you will charge them. But wait, the store has a sale—buy two pairs and get one free—so now you have three pairs of shoes on credit. The shoes cost you 200 bucks. Once the interest starts to kick in on a monthly basis, since you're only paying the minimum due, you end up paying 350 or 400 bucks for those three shoes, which you probably only wear once. So why go buy a pair of shoes you really don't need? To take them home, put them in that overcrowded closet, and never really use them? You are just getting yourself into deeper and deeper debt. If you had cash, you would go in, buy a $50 pair, and call it a day. Zero interest.

A person should own just one card, and it should be left at home for emergency or to make a hotel reservation or rent a car. That's it, not for impulse purchases or I-am-depressed purchases or I-just-have-to-have-a-new-dress purchases.

Go shopping with credit cards. You are only cheating yourself. In the long run, it goes back to you, cutting your paycheck short by needing to pay interest on everything you bought.

CHAPTER 4

Department Store Credit Cards

How would you like to pay for those purchases, cash or credit? You know you can save 10 percent if you sign up for a department store card. *Stop*, don't do it. Your plans were to go into that clothing store, buy $80 worth of clothes, and leave now. You signed up for a department store card, save 10 percent, and you didn't pay for clothing. You kept the $80 and decided to treat yourself with something to eat. After all, you're at the mall and you deserve it. You worked hard. In about a month, you get a bill from the clothing store and you decide, "Let me pay the minimum 'cause I don't have seventy-two bucks right now." The following month, you get another bill, but this time, it has interest on it. Guess what? There goes your 10 percent discount, plus the interest is probably 20 percent, so now you're actually losing money. If you're going to sign up for a department store credit card, after you get your discount, pay your bill at another register. Do not leave that store without paying that bill. Also keep in mind, if you know yourself and you know you can control yourself, that $500 or $1,000 limit they just gave you is going to make you go on a shopping spree. Don't sign up for that card. Say "No, thank you," pay for your purchase, and walk away.

Department stores credit cards are just another way for these clothing stores to take our hard-earned money. You really don't need them. The next time you need a new shirt or shoes or jeans, clean out your closet and you will find plenty to wear, and save your hard-earned money.

CHAPTER 5

ATM Fees

The fees that are charged to you for taking out your money from machines, you can pay anywhere from 50¢ to $10, depending where you took your cash out. And most of the time, you pay twice you pay. The ATM provider 1.50, and your bank charges you a nonbank-use ATM fee as well because you didn't take the cash out from one of their branches. Is this insane or what? Why would you be paying money to take out the money you worked for so hard? It doesn't make any sense whatsoever.

Learn to budget your weekly expenses. Go to your branch and take out the necessary cash so you don't have to go to an ATM and incur crazy fees.

I don't carry an ATM card, so I have extra time to think about impulse purchases. For example, it's 7:00 p.m. and your brother calls you with some emergency. You have no ATM and you have to wait until the next day to go to a branch and withdraw the cash. Well, guess what? By the next morning, either your brother got the cash elsewhere, his emergency disappeared, or you had some time to think about it and decided not to lend him any money. After all, let him get out of his own mess. Why does he always have to call you? Stop paying ATM fees. Take a look at your bank statement on any given month. You could be paying up to twenty bucks of your hard-earned money on ATM fees that are absolutely ridiculous. You can eat lunch a whole week with that twenty bucks, or take your girl out to dinner.

CHAPTER 6

Bank Fees

Nowadays, banks have different fees, ways to charge you, the consumer, money. Now if you don't know this, the banks make money with your money. So why would you need to pay a financial institution a fee to hold your money? If that's the case, keep it in a safe at your house. I refuse to pay any bank fees. As soon as a bank charges me weird fees, I go to another bank. There are still a few banks out there that don't charge any fees. Do some research, and again, save those pennies, save those extra fifteen bucks—fifteen here, fifteen there. They go a long way.

CHAPTER 7

Cell Phone Contracts

Why sign up for a cell phone contract? Because you're getting the cell phone at a discounted price, right? Wrong. Keep in mind that when you sign that two-year contract, you are signing up to pay for that discounted phone three times the average cell phone bill under a contract—it's $125 per month times 24 equals $3,000—while the average prepaid, noncontract, monthly phone bill is $50 times 24 equals $1,200—for a total savings of $1,800. So that $500 phone you got for free or for $100 'cause you signed a two-year contract ends up costing you an average of $1,500 more. The next time you need a cell phone, think $50 unlimited instead of contract. Boost Mobile is the perfect company for this. With the extra $1,500 you saved, take a trip, go shopping, go eating. I'm sure you will think of something.

CHAPTER 8

Vacations on Credit: Time-Shares

Let's begin with time-shares. To me, time-shares are vacations we sign up for that we don't even know if we will take or can take or can afford. Why should I sign up for a time-share where I have to visit the same place every year? Or why would I want but have to pay yearly fees whether I go on vacation or not? Why would you put yourself in a predicament of forcing yourself to go on vacation? Because you are paying a time-share and don't want to lose your money? No no no. I see zero benefits in owning a time-share. No.

When you go on vacation, as soon as you come in, there's always a nice guy or girl offering a free meal or free park tickets. All you have to do is listen to a little offer to one of your time-shares, sit there for two to three hours—that free breakfast could turn out to be the most expensive free breakfast of your life. Say "*No, thanks*. I will pass." They are only trying to sell you a timeshare to there fancy hotel which cost thousands of thousands of dollars.

Taking Vacations on Credit

When you go on vacation on credit is a triple negative. Just think about what you are doing.

1. You are taking time off from work, so you're not making any money.

2. You are charging flights, hotels, car rentals on your credit card.

3. You will have to pay the interest on all those charges you incurred while you were not making any money because you took time off from work.

Triple negative is just insane. Let's stop the we-only-live-once attitude and let's be a little more responsible.

If you're going to go on vacation (and we all deserve to go on vacation), save up the money you will need for the vacation beforehand. So when you come back to work and reality, you don't get hit with an enormous credit card bill and end up paying double for the vacation.

CHAPTER 9

Financing Cars

Financing cars—so you need a car and decided to finance. Great. There is nothing wrong with financing a car. I would prefer you finance a car that is at least six months old so you can save $7K from sticker price. Now, the most important thing is for you to finance a car you are going to stick with for at least fifteen years or twenty years.

Be careful with falling into the never-ending tornado of having to finance a new car every three to five years. You finance a new car in 2005 for $25K. By the year 2007, you're tired of it, and the dealer is sending great offers and a new improved trade-in. Guess what? This improved new trade-in now costs $35K. So you start from scratch instead of almost being finished with your 2005 model. You now have a 2008 model. You owe a lot more money, but at least you are the envy of the block with a brand-new car parked outside your house, even though you haven't even paid for the mirrors yet.

If you continue the trend of trading in your vehicle every three years, you will never have a vehicle that is fully paid for, and you will end up throwing away thousands and thousands of dollars down the drain, paying really expensive prices and interests on these cars. By the year 2011, you traded in one more time and get the improved new model that costs $45K. You get $5K for your 2008 model, and now owe an astonishing $40K with a low, low interest of, let's say, 3 percent. Ask yourself one question: when are you ever going to get out of this cycle? When you turn sixty and retire, or when you don't have a job and can't afford to make the car payments, the tow truck drives it away.

I purchased a new car—a 2002 Toyota—financed for five years, paid a total of $40K after four years. Today is 2012, ten years later. I still have my Toyota, fully paid, and the only things I spent money on are regular maintenance, oils, gas, etc. I have zero car payments since 2007. Now calculate: an average car payment is five hundred bucks, times twelve, is six thousand bucks a year, times last five years, that's $30K savings money. I haven't spent since I have kept the same vehicle for the last ten years.

It looks and drives great. Sure, I would love to have a new convertible BMW parked outside my house, but do I really need it? Do I have other more important things to do with my money, like paying off student loans or credit cards, or saving for my kids' college tuition, or just sending extra cash to my mortgage to try and pay off the house one day? Please think about your next car purchase. Do you really need another $40K debt, another monthly bill to add to your current bills so you can feel more stress? Is the satisfaction of having that new car going to be greater than the stress of having a new car payment?

One day, I woke up and I was like, "I have to get the new white Range Rover. That's it, I worked so hard. I'm almost forty years old. I deserve a big-ticket purchase." I went online, I built it, and then I saw my monthly payment is nine hundred bucks. I was like, "Wow, shit. I won't be able to go on vacation if I get this Rover." So guess what I did?

Got it anyway, stretched myself. Nope, no, nope.

I painted my car from black to white, and I called my Toyota a Rover. Spent a total of 2,500 bucks, and I have a brand-new car and zero car payments.

CHAPTER 10

Bill-Me-Later Furniture Purchases

How about the new furniture offers where you can take your living room set, bedroom set, dining room set home today, in the year 2012, and start paying for it in the year 2015? And guess what? By the year 2015, when you get that bill to start paying for that furniture, you don't even want it anymore. It's old and broken and you are already thinking about getting new furniture, and now, you have to pay for this old furniture with interest. Doesn't make any sense whatsoever. If you can't afford it, don't rent it, don't take it on credit. Save up the cash and pay for it in full.

CHAPTER 11

Student Loans

So you are off to college and can't afford to pay for your tuition. You don't have a scholarship and your parents don't have any cash. What to do?

Before you decide to go to a prestigious college with a bunch of fees, think, "Am I really going to practice law after I graduate?" or "Am I really going to be a doctor or a nurse or whatever degree I decided to get from this expensive school?" Those student loans have to be paid off eventually? And guess what? The interest rate kicks in eventually. Do you really want to finish college and owe more than $50K? Don't you think you will have a lot of stress, knowing you have to work for five years or more to pay this money back? I think it is better if you go to a community college and the only cost you have to pay is $20K in loans when you finish college. The statistics show that less than half of college students actually go to work in their chosen fields. Therefore, be very careful in choosing a lucrative, big name.

School—getting a real nice degree that you will never use but still be responsible to pay thousands of dollars in student loans for a very long time with interest.

CHAPTER 12

Home Interest Rates

The only purchase you should be paying interest on is your home because of how much a home costs, and because it is the single most important purchase in your entire life.

Now, even though I am okay with you having to pay interest to purchase your home, I need you to try and get the best possible interest and get a fixed fifteen-year or thirty-year mortgage, not an adjustable mortgage or one with a ballon payment. Be careful with buying a house that's too expensive for you. You don't want to be house poor were you have a nice mansion you really can't afford. Don't bite off more than you can chew. Don't live a life where you're working just to pay the bills or make ends meet.

You want to purchase a house with mortgage payments that can be paid by one of the breadwinners. Just in case the other one gets sick, you can still afford to pay your mortgage and keep your house.

When purchasing a home, keep in mind that the price you paid for the house will always be with you while the interest in the housing market will continue to change with the times. Example, I would rather you purchase a house for less than $400K with a high interest rate of 7 percent than you purchase a house for $600K with an interest of only 4 percent. In the long run, you will have a lot more money to pay the $600K house versus the $400K house, and eventually, the housing market will shift and the interest will go down. At which time, you can refinance for a lower rate and still only owe $400K you started with.

Today is May 2012, and in a weird twist, the housing prices are low and the interests are low also. It is definitely a buyer's market, but be careful. Take your time. Make good, sound decisions. This isn't an apartment you're renting where you can move in a flash if you're not happy with something. It is a house you decided to purchase, with the thought of living there for five, ten, thirty years.

Make sure you shop the neighborhood for schools, crimes, neighbors, shops, traffic, and convenience. Make sure you can afford the mortgage taxes and utility bills with no problem. Finally, buy your house, and good luck.

CHAPTER 13

Refinancing Your Home to Do Repairs: Pay Off Loans, Car Loans, Vacations, or Credit Cards

Okay, so you have your home and you have been paying your monthly mortgage for five to ten years, and you have accrued a little equity and you want to refinance your house to pay your car loan, your vacations, your credit card bills, your student loan. Great idea? No. Nope. Nooooo.

What do you think is going to happen if you refinance your house and pay off your bills? The first few days, you are going to feel relieved. Then when you get your first mortgage payment with a new payment amount, you are going to get stressed. Also you have just told yourself, "It's okay to run up your credit cards, it's okay to finance cars you really can't afford, it's okay to go on vacations with credit vacations you really can't afford." Do not get yourself into a mess of debt and think refinancing your house is the solution. How are you supposed to ever finish paying off your home if you continue to refinance every five years? Please do not refinance your house unless you have a near-death experience.

Finally, we need to stay away from interest. We need to purchase things with cash only.

You want to get ahead, you want to give yourself a raise, you want to make more money. Well, stop paying ATM fees and stop using credit cards, financing new cars every year, going on vacations you can't afford, and you will be getting ahead real fast. For if you don't ever pay interest, your money will buy more—it will be worth more; you will be stretching your paycheck and maximizing its return.

Do you really think the banks need more of our money? Do you really think it takes a magician to figure this all out? We need to have willpower and strength and sacrifice and start saving and spending when we really need to. We need to stop the impulse purchase, and we need to differentiate our wants from our needs. The sooner we get rid of that I-want list, the sooner we will start saving and becoming happier and more financially free.

Have a great day.

Supa Dave

ABOUT ME

Raymond Vasquez, a.k.a. Supa Dave, is a young father, husband, friend, entrepreneur, salesman, scholar, Renaissance man. I am thirty-nine years old, and I have been running my own business since I was twenty-two years old.

I strongly believe in establishing lifetime relationships. I have owned the same vehicle for ten years, have been together with same woman for fifteen years, and have been running my business for seventeen years. Stay within the course—stay focused, consistent, disciplined, ambitious—sacrifice, lay your foundation properly and strongly, and God will pay you back one thousand times.

ABOUT THE BOOK

The thought that credit is the devil is exactly the message I want you to take from this book, *Plastic Devil*.

I want all consumers, especially the younger generation, to read this book before they decide to go shopping on credit, before they make a purchase they don't really need.

Before you get into a never-ending, out-of-control credit card debt cycle, read this book.

Credit cards, department store cards, ATM fees, bank fees, bill-me-later furniture deals, student loans, car interest rates—all these forms of credits and fees are things that will and can ruin our lives forever.

INDEX